I0605537

CANINE CONNECTION

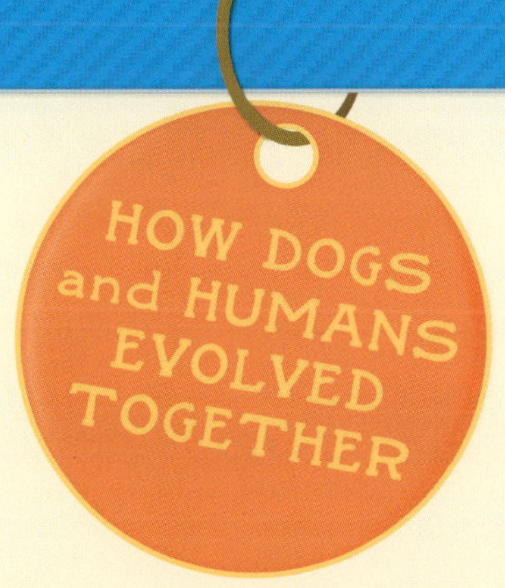

CHRISTOPHER GUDGEON

ORCA BOOK PUBLISHERS

Published in Canada and the United States in 2025 by Orca Book Publishers.
orcabook.com

Library and Archives Canada Cataloguing in Publication
Title: Canine connection : how dogs and humans evolved together / Christopher Gudgeon.
Names: Gudgeon, Christopher, 1959- author
Series: Orca wild ; 18.
Description: Series statement: Orca wild ; 18 | Includes bibliographical references and index.
Identifiers: Canadiana (print) 20240484975 | Canadiana (ebook) 20240484991 | ISBN 9781459839496 (hardcover) | ISBN 9781459839502 (PDF) | ISBN 9781459839519 (EPUB)
Subjects: LCSH: Dogs—History—Juvenile literature. | LCSH: Dogs—Evolution—Juvenile literature. | LCSH: Human-animal relationships—Juvenile literature.
Classification: LCC SF422.5 .G83 2025 | DDC j636.7009—dc23

Library of Congress Control Number: 2024946779

Summary: Part of the nonfiction Orca Wild series for middle-grade readers and illustrated with color photographs throughout, this book will help young readers explore the relationship between dogs and humans, and how their bond has evolved throughout history.

Orca Book Publishers is committed to reducing the consumption of nonrenewable resources in the production of our books. We make every effort to use materials that support a sustainable future.

Orca Book Publishers gratefully acknowledges the support for its publishing programs provided by the following agencies: the Government of Canada, the Canada Council for the Arts and the Province of British Columbia through the BC Arts Council and the Book Publishing Tax Credit.

Front cover photo by Mexitographer/iStock/Getty Images Plus.
Back cover photo by darrya/iStock/Getty Images Plus.
Design by Troy Cunningham.
Edited by Kirstie Hudson.

Printed and bound in South Korea.

28 27 26 25 • 1 2 3 4

REBECCA NELSON/GETTY IMAGES

To Elvis,
who lives forever
in my heart.

CONTENTS

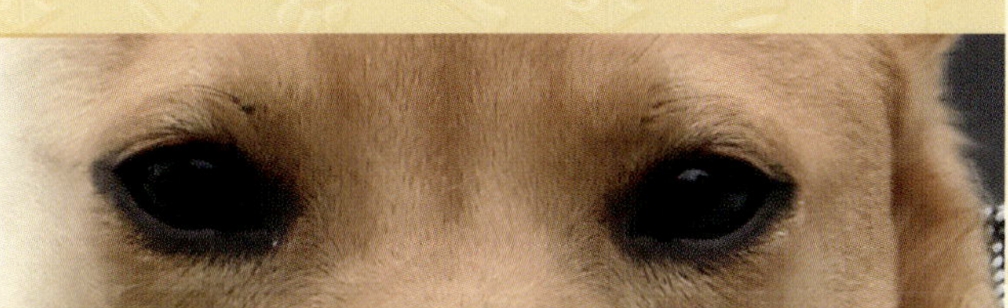

A black Lab just like Elvis.
JOSEPHGRUBER/GETTY IMAGES

Introduction

MY BFF, ELVIS

If I made a list of the closest friends I've had in my whole life, near the very top would be the name Elvis. Before you get the wrong idea, Elvis was a dog. And not just any dog. He was a wonderful, loving, sensitive, goofy black Lab and one of my best friends ever.

I got him just out of high school. I didn't have a job or a plan for my life. I didn't really have any close friends. One day a neighbor asked me if I wanted a dog. Her sister's black Lab had just had puppies, and they'd all been sold or adopted except one. He was the runt of the litter—skinny, sickly and shy. Nobody wanted him.

I wasn't sure I wanted a puppy. I was having a hard enough time taking care of myself. The neighbor suggested I take the dog for a sleepover. If I decided I didn't want him, she'd take him back, no questions asked.

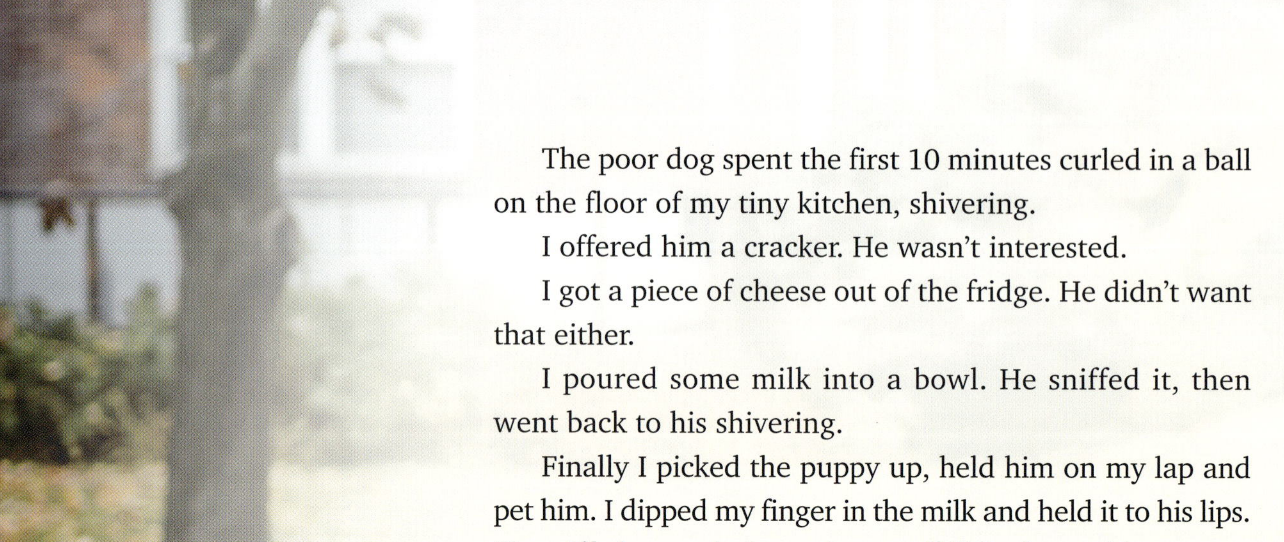

The poor dog spent the first 10 minutes curled in a ball on the floor of my tiny kitchen, shivering.

I offered him a cracker. He wasn't interested.

I got a piece of cheese out of the fridge. He didn't want that either.

I poured some milk into a bowl. He sniffed it, then went back to his shivering.

Finally I picked the puppy up, held him on my lap and pet him. I dipped my finger in the milk and held it to his lips. He sniffed tentatively, took a small lick, then a bigger one. Next thing I knew, he was lapping milk from my cupped hand.

That night I made a nest of blankets at the end of the bed and stroked the puppy's head until he fell asleep. When I woke up the next morning, he was under the covers, snuggled close beside me.

IT WAS LOVE

After that, Elvis—the name came to me in a dream—and I were best friends. He came to know my moods and thoughts almost instinctively, just as I knew his. It occurred to me how strange it was that two creatures from such different worlds could understand each other so completely.

I began to wonder, even way back then, why it is that humans and dogs get along so well. In fact, Elvis and I did more than just "get along." I loved Elvis and was sure in my heart that he loved me too.

Elvis is long gone, sadly. But it always makes me happy to remember him. I never stopped wondering what connects dogs and humans so perfectly. When I talked to other people, I was surprised to find that they wondered the same thing.

And that's how this book came about. *Canine Connection* explores the magical relationship between dogs and their people. Turns out it's not just a fluke. Our ***species*** has had thousands of years to work on this friendship, and if you ask me, I'd say we've pretty much perfected it.

Dogs and kids—
best friends forever!
CAVAN IMAGES/GETTY IMAGES

Who's your favorite dog friend?
RYANJLANE/GETTY IMAGES

DOGS AND THEIR HUMANS, FRIENDS FOREVER

They are friendly, furry bundles of love. Maybe you have one in your home. A golden retriever or beagle. A giant-sized St. Bernard or an itsy-bitsy Chihuahua. Maybe she's just a good old-fashioned mutt, Misty or Rex or Rover or Buttons. What breed is she? Who cares? All that matters is that she's affectionate and loyal—and loves to cuddle.

Even if you don't own a dog, you probably know someone who does. Maybe your aunt has a stylish shar-pei. Or your next-door neighbors have an old German shepherd named Otto, and every once in a while, when you're bored, your neighbors let you take him to the park to play fetch. Perhaps your best friend since kindergarten has a purebred chow chow, regal and dignified, with papers that trace her ***pedigree*** back 15 generations.

A DOG IS A DOG IS A DOG...

It can be big or small or somewhere in between, black or white or brown or red, if it has fur at all. Do its ears stand straight up? Flop to the sides? A little of both? No matter what your favorite looks like, it's a member of the same family. It's a dog, and they've been humanity's best buds since—literally—the dawn of time.

And what a friendship it is. There are 150 to 300 million pet dogs in the world today, some 80 million in the United States alone and another 8 million in Canada. It's a world in which:

74 percent of people consider their dog a full member of the family;

78 percent buy their dogs birthday and Christmas gifts; and

a whopping 80 percent of people regularly share their beds with their favorite pooch pal(s).

Talk about strange bedfellows—when it comes to the animal kingdom, the relationship between dogs and humans is as weird and wonderful as it gets.

Dogs were made for cuddling.
CAVAN IMAGES/GETTY IMAGES

DOG STATS AND FACTS

SCIENTIFIC NAME: *Canis lupus familiaris* (the Latin *Canis* means "dog," *lupus* means "wolf" and *familiaris* means "belonging to a family").

RANGE: Everywhere there are humans.

SPECIES: One species (300–400 breeds).

LIFESPAN: 10–13 years, depending on the breed. French mastiffs have the shortest average lifespan, at 5–8 years. Chihuahuas and shih tzus, with a range of about 12–16 years, are the longest lived. Bobi, a Rafeiro do Alentejo (a Portuguese herding dog), died in 2023 at the age of 31 years and 165 days. He is oldest dog on record.

SIZE: Breed size varies greatly, as dogs are the most diverse species of all mammals.

- **SMALLEST BREED IS THE CHIHUAHUA:** Average height at withers (shoulder), 6–9 inches (15–30 centimeters); length, 9.5–15 inches (24–38 centimeters); weight, 3–6 pounds (1.4–2.7 kilograms).
- **BIGGEST BREED IS THE GREAT DANE:** Average height, 28–32 inches (71–81 centimeters); length, 35–43 inches (90–109 centimeters); weight, 110–175 pounds (50–79 kilograms).

(TOP) SUWINAI SUKANANT/ GETTY IMAGES; (BOTTOM) CAPUSKI/ GETTY IMAGES

REPRODUCTION: A female dog can have up to three litters a year, with an average of five to six puppies per litter.

DIET: Dogs are omnivorous and eat pretty much whatever humans eat. Be careful, though. Chocolate, avocado, garlic, macadamia nuts, grapes and some other foods can make your dog very sick. Check with your veterinarian to find out which foods are safe.

CHARACTERISTICS: Playful, loyal, people-loving, pack- or family-oriented.

THREAT TO HUMANS: Dogs usually get along great with humans. But packs of wild or stray dogs have been known to attack humans. The biggest threat is if a dog has contracted rabies.

Look at that irresistible face. Say "cheese"!
COROIMAGE/GETTY IMAGES

IT'S IN OUR GENES

Social media is full of them—pics of Frenchies and Yorkies and black Labs, looking right at the camera and so cute you just want to pick them up and cuddle them. They've got their heads tilted just so, their eyebrows raised and eyes wide open as they stare lovingly at us (or, at least, at the last bite of hamburger we're about to eat). It's that irresistible face—one our ***canine*** companions are experts at using on us humans.

But here's the thing. It's no accident. According to a 2019 study headed by Juliane Kaminski of the University of Portsmouth, UK, it's actually ***evolution*** at work. It turns out that over the course of thousands of years, the muscles around dogs' eyes have changed in very specific ways to help them communicate better with humans. In other words, when your bichon frise looks at you with her puppy-dog eyes, her childlike expression isn't just a fluke. It's an evolutionary adaption allowing an inner eyebrow movement that makes the eyes look larger and like a human toddler's. It's a move designed to trigger a nurturing response and strengthen the emotional bond between humans and dogs.

A SHARED JOURNEY

Yup, those puppy-dog eyes are the result of dogs and humans living together for thousands and thousands of years. During that time, we humans have become adept at understanding dog speak, the sounds and ***body language*** that tell us when our four-legged friends want to have dinner or play fetch or go outside to pee. A wagging tail? That dog's happy to see you. Head lowered and snarling? That dog means trouble.

As for dogs, these once wild and wandering canines, former vicious predators, have morphed into docile homebodies. They're smaller and more outgoing than their ancient ancestors, their ears are less perky, their tails a little floppier—all signs of obedience in the canine world. Even their fur has changed, becoming softer and better suited to snuggling.

Once wild predators, now happy homebodies.
FOTYMA/GETTY IMAGES

PARLEZ-VOUS POOCH?

How good are you at reading a dog's body language? Here are a few tell-tail (pun intended) signs of what your pooch is trying to tell you.

- **TAIL TALK:** A wagging tail doesn't always mean a happy dog. A high wag might show excitement or joy, while a low wag could mean uncertainty or caution.
- **EARS UP, EARS DOWN:** When their ears are perked up, dogs are usually alert and interested. If the ears are flat against their head, it might signal fear or submission.
- **EYE CONTACT:** Staring can be a sign of dominance or aggression, so a soft gaze usually means your dog feels safe and friendly.
- **SMILE OR SNARL:** Dogs show their teeth for different reasons. A relaxed, open-mouthed grin often means happiness, while bared teeth can mean they're upset.
- **BODY POSTURE:** A confident, relaxed dog stands tall with a loose body. If they crouch low or try to make themselves small, they might be anxious or scared.
- **YAWNING AND LIP LICKING:** These behaviors can signal stress or discomfort, especially in unfamiliar situations.
- **HACKLES RAISED:** When the fur along a dog's back stands up, it usually means they're feeling threatened or aggressive.
- **PLAY BOW:** This classic move involves a lowered front with the rear end up, and it's an invitation to play and have fun.

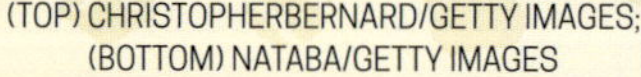

(TOP) CHRISTOPHERBERNARD/GETTY IMAGES; (BOTTOM) NATABA/GETTY IMAGES

Dogs have also taken a page from the human book, becoming experts in our body language. They are particularly aware of our facial expressions and eye movement. In fact, a study by researchers in Hong Kong found that dogs can tell the difference between angry and happy human faces. A happy face makes a dog feel good. An angry face stresses out the dog. Even a simple eye movement speaks volumes to a dog. They carefully watch our every move to figure what we're thinking. Look one way, it could mean a walk in the park. Look another, it might mean it's dreaded bath time!

Dogs can move and raise their eyebrows, just like us.
DEVON OPDENDRIES/GETTY IMAGES

Dogs have also adapted to the human diet. Unlike their wild wolf counterparts, who are mostly ***carnivorous***, modern dogs have ***enzymes*** that allow them to digest the fruits, grains, vegetables and other weird things human love to eat.

FOREVER YOUNG

The biggest change of all? Dogs have undergone a complete personality makeover. They're still sociable and cooperative (like wolves), but friendlier and locked in a kind of endless puppyhood. They love to play, frolic and cuddle (things adult wolves rarely do). Being more puppy-like than their wild cousins makes it even easier for us humans to love them.

In fact, dog faces have even changed over time to appeal to us more. Their eyes became larger and rounder, and they developed muscles that allowed them to raise their eyebrows and widen their eyes. This makes them look more like human children, which makes us want to love them even more.

Why do we love dogs so much?

The answer seems obvious. Dogs are perfect companions. Loving, caring, playful, a little goofy, loyal as all get-out—dogs are everything you look for in a BFF. But don't just take my word for it. Science confirms that we humans are happier and healthier when we have dogs in our lives. A few minutes cuddling with your favorite canine can slow your heart rate and fill your brain with oxytocin, a special ***hormone*** that makes you feel calm and connected (in fact, it's the same hormone that bonds mothers to their babies).

But the real secret to the relationship is that we've been working on it for so long, we've had lots of time to get it right.

Loving, caring, playful and a little goofy—these are some of the characteristics that make dogs lovable.
ALDOMURILLO/GETTY IMAGES

A long time ago humans were nomadic hunters.
ESTT/GETTY IMAGES

HARD TIMES

How long? We're talking way, way back, before the pyramids were built or the wheel was invented, before people lived in cities or farmed, during what scientists call the ***Paleolithic*** period, which was roughly 2.6 million to 11,700 years ago.

Life was hard. Earth was in the grip of the last Ice Age. Glaciers covered a quarter of the world, and the average temperature was 18 degrees Fahrenheit (10 degrees Celsius) lower than it is today. We humans lived as ***nomadic*** hunters and gatherers, spending our days tracking down big mammals, like mammoths and woolly rhinoceroses, or collecting roots, berries and seeds. At night we slept in caves, temporary huts, portable tepees and open fields. Disease and starvation were everywhere—few of our Paleolithic ancestors lived to see their 30th birthday.

THE ICE AGES

The ice ages were long periods in Earth's history when large parts of the planet were covered in glaciers and snow. These chilly episodes occurred over millions of years and shaped our world in remarkable ways. During these periods, vast glaciers spread out from the North and South Poles, advancing and retreating in cycles that lasted hundreds of thousands of years. The icy intrusion helped shape the way the earth looks, carving deep valleys and gorges, shifting huge boulders hundreds of miles and helping create lakes, rivers and streams.

The last Ice Age started 2.4 million years ago and lasted until about 11,500 years ago. That means both modern humans and our dog BFFs evolved during the harsh ice-age climate.

An ancient petroglyph showing the oldest known image of a dog.

Things were so bad that by the time the Ice Age ended, there were only about 1,200 ***Homo sapiens*** left. The entire world's population could have easily fit in an average high school gym. Humanity was on the brink of extinction.

PREHISTORIC PET PIC

Back in the mid-2010s, archaeologists excavating two sites in northwestern Saudi Arabia made a remarkable discovery. The sites are full of ancient petroglyphs—drawings scratched deep into the sandstone cliffs. Among the 1,400 or so pictures the archaeologists found, one stood out. It showed a hunter drawing his bow, ready to shoot an unseen prey. Surrounding him were 11 dogs, including two leashed and tied to the hunter's waist. The petroglyphs are over 8,000 years old, making the hunter and his posse of pooches the oldest artistic portrayal of dogs ever discovered.

MYSTERIOUS BEGINNINGS

Despite the hardships, we achieved a lot. We figured out how to make and use stone tools— things like axes, hammers and knives—and unlocked the secret of fire. We invented music, painting, weaving and other art forms. We also started hanging out with friendly, intelligent, four-legged animals—smaller, nicer versions of the wolf, one of our main competitors for mammoth meat.

When and where dogs and humans first got together, nobody knows for sure. In fact, scientists wildly disagree. Some say it was 10,000 years ago. Some say 20,000. Some think it goes back 40,000 years or more.

Did the dog-human friendship begin in what is now Europe? East Asia? The Middle East?

Did it happen once? Twice? Multiple times?

The questions remain unanswered. What we do know is that at some forgotten point in time, in some forgotten place, *Homo sapiens* and wild canines formed an unlikely cross-species alliance that might have just changed the course of history.

Humans and dogs have an unlikely cross-species alliance that changed the course of history.
WESTEND61/GETTY IMAGES

Dogs and humans have evolved to love each other.
ANDRESR/GETTY IMAGES

TALKING 'BOUT EVOLUTION

As we learned in the previous chapter, dogs are experts at reading body language and facial expressions. In fact, they are much better at reading us than even our closest animal relatives, chimpanzees, are. But why are they so good at understanding us? The big reason is because the two species have evolved together over tens of thousands of years. This ***coevolution***, as scientists call it, has helped create two species biologically programmed to get along.

Evolution is the natural process that explains how living things develop over a long period of time. The basic idea behind evolution is that species adapt a tiny bit at a time in response to various changes in their environment. Over a long period these small changes add up to something much bigger.

Billions of years ago, when life first started on Earth, you'd find only simple single-celled organisms. All living things have evolved from these humble beginnings, from the one-celled whatchamacallits to humans, with our 30 trillion ***cells*** and counting!

DARWIN'S NATURAL SELECTION

The key to evolution is something the famous 19th-century scientist Charles Darwin called "natural selection." This is the idea that organisms with the traits best suited to their environment have the greatest chance of surviving and passing those traits to the next generation. Over hundreds of generations, the useful traits become more common in the population and often help define the species.

This beagle shares a name with the ship Charles Darwin sailed on to the Galápagos Islands, the HMS *Beagle.*

CATHERINE FALLS COMMERCIAL/ GETTY IMAGES

Take the arctic fox. A distant relative of the dog, this fox has a coat that becomes thick and white during the harsh northern winter. This trait has a number of benefits, including keeping the foxes warm in the winter and helping camouflage them from both predators and prey.

Long ago most of these foxes probably had a brown coat all year long. Only a few had the white-fur ***mutation***. But over time, foxes with a white winter coat were more likely to survive, giving them a greater chance of passing on the white-winter-coat ***genes***.

Fast-forward several thousand years, and now all arctic foxes have white winter coats. What started off as a fluke is an essential trait now that defines the species and helps ensure its long-term survival.

The arctic fox is a distant relative of the dog.
JEAN LANDRY/GETTY IMAGES

BIRDS OF A FEATHER (EVOLVE TOGETHER)

Evolution doesn't just happen within a species. Sometimes two species sharing the same ***habitat*** evolve together, developing shared or complementary traits that help both species survive. There are lots of examples of coevolution in nature. Take the relationship between the humble honeybee and its favorite flower. The bee needs to drink the flower's nectar—its main food source—to survive. The flower needs the bee to spread its pollen to other flowers so it can reproduce. And so certain flowers evolved to bee (sorry) the right color and perfect scent to attract the best bees. Those bees in turn evolved to be attracted to that flower's color and scent and have bee-come (sorry!) the exact right size (with just the right amount of stickiness to their legs) to fit inside the flower and collect its pollen.

DARWIN AND EVOLUTION

Charles Darwin was a famous scientist who changed the way we think about life on Earth. Born in England in 1809, Darwin became curious about nature at a young age. In 1831, when he was just 22 years old, Darwin got a job as ***naturalist*** on the HMS *Beagle*, a British ship embarking on a long scientific journey to find new plants and animals. One place the ship stopped was the remote Galápagos Islands in the South Pacific. The islands were famous for the unique plants and animals that thrived there, things not found anywhere else on Earth.

Darwin noticed that the beaks of certain birds were different from island to island. It occurred to him that maybe their beaks had evolved over time to help them eat specific types of food available on each island. This started Darwin thinking about evolution, eventually leading him to develop the idea of natural selection and that all species of life have evolved over time from common ancestors. His ideas help us understand the amazing diversity of life on Earth and how species, including dogs and humans, adapt to their environments.

Bees and flowers work together.
ANTON PETRUS/GETTY IMAGES

EVOLUTION TIMES TWO

Then there are aphids and ants, who've taken cross-species cooperation to a whole different level! Aphids are small sap-sucking insects that feed on the juices of plants. They're not very good at defending themselves from predators like ladybirds and wasps. Ants are known for their teamwork and intelligence. They also have a weakness for sweet treats like flower nectar and something called honeydew, a sugary liquid that aphids produce as they feed on plant juices.

Ants team up to protect aphids from their natural enemies (and even move them to the juiciest part of the plant). In return, aphids give them all the delicious honeydew they can handle. Ants are even known to "milk" their aphid livestock, gently stroking them with their antennae to encourage them to release more honeydew.

Coevolution isn't limited to what scientists call ***mutualistic relationships***, where two species (like our bee and flower) cooperate to help one another. Predators and prey often evolve together. As predators develop new hunting strategies, prey change in ways that help them evade capture.

The back-and-forth between cheetahs and gazelles is a good example. As cheetahs evolved to become faster, more agile hunters, gazelles kept pace. The result? Today both species produce incredible athletes. Cheetahs are the fastest land animal, reaching top speeds of 70 miles (113 kilometers) per hour. Some species of gazelles, meanwhile, can run almost as fast as cheetahs—60 miles (100 kilometers) per hour. They are the champion jumpers of the animal kingdom, able to leap 10 feet (3 meters) into the air and up to 33 feet (10 meters) forward. This gives them a fighting chance against those fleet-footed cheetahs.

MORE COEVOLVED SPECIES

Dogs and humans, ants and aphids—these aren't the only species that get along well. Nature is full of coevolved cooperators.

- **OXPECKERS AND LARGE MAMMALS:** Oxpeckers are birds that often hitch rides on large mammals like rhinos, buffalo and giraffes. In return, the birds eat ticks and other parasites from the mammals' skin.
- **NILE CROCODILES AND EGYPTIAN PLOVERS:** Likewise, Egyptian plovers are small birds that feed on bits of food stuck in the teeth of Nile crocodiles. The crocodiles allow the birds to approach their open mouths without harming them.
- **GOBI DESERT CAMELS AND WILD WOLVES:** In the harsh Gobi Desert, wild Bactrian camels have been observed living near packs of wolves. Camels are vigilant and can spot predators, while the wolves help protect the camels from threats.
- **PILOT FISH AND SHARKS:** Pilot fish swim alongside sharks, cleaning up scraps of food left behind from the shark's meals. They help the shark by picking parasites off its skin.

As cheetahs got faster, gazelles became more agile.
WINFRIED WISNIEWSKI/GETTY IMAGES

DID NEANDERTHALS HAVE DOGS?

Neanderthals were a species of early hominoids and a close relative of modern humans. Both species lived in parts of France and Spain, an overlapping existence that lasted from 54,000 years ago to about 2,600 years ago. The two species definitely came into contact with each other. In fact, if you have any European ancestors, you probably have a few Neanderthal genes kicking around in your ***DNA.***

We certainly know that there were dogs around in those days, and humans were already keeping them as helpers and companions. But did Neanderthals also have a bond with dogs? The answer is a resounding... maybe. Archaeologists have found ancient sites where Neanderthal and dog footprints overlap. But there's no hard evidence, like the dog bones found in human burial sites. Maybe one day we'll have an answer. Right now only the Neanderthals know for sure...and they aren't saying much!

YOU SCRATCH MY EARS, I'LL LICK YOURS

Coevolution can also involve host species and the parasite species that live off them. Think of those pictures you've seen of giant sperm or gray whales with hundreds of tiny shells called barnacles attached to their skin. Barnacles use a strong cement-like substance to give themselves a moving home that helps them feed on floating plankton.

But barnacles are parasites, and while they might provide some benefits to their hosts (such as giving whales greater buoyancy and camouflage), they can cause problems. Too many barnacles on a whale can slow it down or irritate the whale's skin, increasing the chance of infection.

Just like bees and flowers, aphids and ants, and even gray whales and their scratchy passengers, dogs and humans benefit from their coevolutionary relationship. But how do the two species help each other survive? For early humans, dogs were great to have around. They helped in the hunt, using their powerful sense of smell to track prey more effectively than we humans ever could. They used their speed, cooperative skills and natural aggressiveness to help us capture and kill our prey. They guarded us against predators and hostile ***hominoids***, using their sensitive hearing and built-in wariness to help protect us. They were always ready to bark a warning or, snarling with teeth bared, attack an unwanted intruder.

With dogs helping us find food and keeping us safe at night, humans were able to survive and thrive while all the other hominoids—like the Neanderthals—

Dogs and humans help one another in a lot of ways.
MAICA/GETTY IMAGES

became extinct. In return for their help, dogs got easier access to food, protection from their natural enemies and the kind of loving attention few creatures ever receive in the wild. It's the perfect relationship, where both partners give a little but get a lot in return.

MEET THE WORLD'S OLDEST DOG BREED

Cross a husky with a fox and you have an idea of what a Shiba Inu looks like. It's a beautiful, powerful dog that many people believe is the oldest surviving dog breed on Earth. How old? In the early 1960s archaeologists found two Shiba Inu bones at a dig in the Japanese mountains. ***Carbon dating*** showed that the bones were about 9,400 years old. The Shiba Inu's ancestors originated in the Japanese mountains, where they were bred to hunt wild boar, elk and other large game.

ISRAEL SEBASTIAN/GETTY IMAGES

Are dogs just domesticated wolves?
STAFFAN WIDSTRAND/GETTY IMAGES

A DOG IN WOLF'S CLOTHING

Not so long ago, most scientists believed that modern dogs were directly descended from gray wolves. The thinking was that, one way or another, we humans encountered wolves and realized they were good at things like hunting and guarding. So we decided to domesticate them and make them a permanent part of our lives.

Domestication is the process of taming wild plants and animals to make them a useful part of the human world. Take plants, for example. Thousands of years ago, humans began experimenting with wild plants to figure out which ones could best be used for food. People selected their favorite plants and selectively bred them into the biggest, healthiest, tastiest crops. Fruits, vegetables and grains like wheat, corn and barley are only some of the plants that humans have domesticated.

How did early humans and dogs first get together?
CLU/GETTY IMAGES

HISTORY'S GREATEST LOVE AFFAIR

Humans domesticated other animals too. At some point our ancient ancestors realized that instead of going out hunting for animals, it would be easier to keep them nearby. An ongoing supply of cows and goats meant ready access to meat, milk, cheese, bones (for munching and tools) and skins (for making clothes). But there's no doubt that dogs were the first thing we ever domesticated—and by a long shot. As for exactly how this happened, though, scientists weren't sure. There were two popular theories about how history's greatest love affair went down.

The curious wolf ***theory***. Once upon a time, a curious wolf wandered into a human camp to get a better look at what all the fire and fuss were about. Somebody threw the wolf a scrap of meat, and the wolf kept coming back for more until it built up a wary bond with the humans.

The pity-the-poor-puppy theory. Also once upon a time, some wandering hominoids were out for a day's forage when they stumbled across an orphaned wolf pup. They felt sorry for the animal, brought it home, fed and cared for it. Following this chance meeting, both the dog and its human caretakers realized there were benefits to the relationship.

WOLF STATS AND FACTS

SCIENTIFIC NAME: *Canis lupus* (the Latin words for "dog" and "wolf").

RANGE: Parts of North America, Europe, Asia, India, the Middle East and Africa.

SPECIES: Two (or three) species: gray, red and maybe timber (which some scientists think is a separate species, while others say it is a subspecies of grays). There are 38 subspecies.

LIFESPAN: Six to eight years in the wild. In captivity, wolves have been known to live up to 16 years.

SIZE: The average adult male gray wolf stands 30 inches (76 centimeters) tall at the shoulder and weighs about 100 pounds (45 kilograms). Females are slightly smaller.

REPRODUCTION: The members of a wolf pack carefully control its population. An entire pack normally produces only one litter of four to six puppies a year.

DIET: Most wolves are carnivores, preying on large ***herbivores*** like deer, elk, moose and reindeer.

CHARACTERISTICS: Community-based animals, living in packs with up to 30 members. Highly effective and organized hunters.

NATURFOTO HONAL/GETTY IMAGES

THREAT TO HUMANS: Wolf attacks on humans are very rare and usually only happen if the animal has rabies.

TWO PEAS IN A PACK

It makes sense that people would think dogs evolved from gray wolves. The two species share 99 percent of their DNA, the chemical blueprint encoded into the genes of all living things. The more DNA two species have in common, the more closely related they are.

With so much shared DNA, it's no wonder dogs and wolves have a lot of physical and character traits in common.

This Great Pyrenees loves guarding her flock.
HARPAZO_HOPE/GETTY IMAGES

For one thing, wolves are known for their tightly knit social groups, called packs, and dogs show similar social behavior. Both animals thrive in groups and rely on cooperation within their pack or human family for survival and companionship.

Also, dogs and wolves use similar body language and vocalizations, like barks, howls and whimpers, and can more or less understand each other. Both wolves and dogs are territorial animals, which means they know how big their home turf is and will fight to protect it. This sense of property and boundaries is what make dogs good guard animals.

Wolves are also skilled predators and are great at working together on the hunt. Dogs may have lost some of their edge when it comes to hunting, but they are still pretty effective. With their amazing sense of smell, their focused hearing, innate aggressiveness and awesome teamwork skills, certain breeds—like Labs, spaniels and bloodhounds—make great hunting partners.

ALL IN THE FAMILY

Another reason scientists thought dogs were descended from wolves was that the two species can easily ***crossbreed***. And not only can dogs and wolves have puppies together, but those puppies are ***fertile*** and capable of producing offspring of their own. This isn't always the case with crossbred species. Dogs and foxes are close cousins, but it's extremely rare for them to interbreed (there's only one known case of a dog-fox hybrid). Likewise, cats and lions are members of the same family but have zero chance of successfully mating (can you imagine the litter box if they did!).

(LEFT) ONFOKUS/GETTY IMAGES; (RIGHT) ALISON LUND

MUTTS ADO ABOUT SOMETHING

Sometimes crossbreeding occurs in the natural world. Polar bears and grizzlies, for example, have been known to interbreed in regions where their ranges overlap due to climate change and habitat loss. The resulting hybrids, known as "pizzly bears" or "grolar bears," have a blend of characteristics (size, body shape, fur color) from both parent species.

Humans often crossbreed species to produce specific traits. For example, a farmer will deliberately breed a male donkey and female horse to produce a mule, which combines the strength and endurance of a donkey with the size and speed of a horse.

A cross between a polar bear and grizzly bear. Pizzly bear? Grolar?

PHILIPPE CLEMENT/ GETTY IMAGES

AND NOT SO SIMILAR...

Despite all the similarities, there are key differences between dogs and wolves.

- **BEHAVIOR:** Wolves live in packs and have a strong hierarchical structure. Dogs have adapted to living with humans. They are friendly, loyal and often form strong bonds with their owners.
- **LOOKS:** Wolves are usually larger and stronger than dogs, with thicker fur, sharper facial features and bushy tails. Dogs come in various shapes and sizes, depending on their breed, and their appearance can vary greatly.
- **VOCALIZATIONS:** While dogs and wolves can communicate with each other, dogs are programmed to pay attention to humans and are experts at reading our body language. Wolves are wary of humans and do not pay close attention to how we communicate.
- **DIET:** Wolves are, for the most part, carnivores. Dogs have a wider diet, heavily influenced by their life with humans.
- **HUMAN INTERACTION:** Dogs are our faithful friends, eager to please, and they often seek our attention and approval. Wolves are wild and cautious, keep their distance from humans and couldn't care less about being our friends.

DOX? FOG? HOW ABOUT DOGXIM?

In 2001 a Brazilian researcher came across a strange creature. The animal had been hit by a car, and a passing motorist brought it into an animal hospital. In some ways it looked like a small dog, but it had a foxlike head, wiry fur and bushy tail. Stranger still, it liked to climb bushes, something dogs don't normally do, and refused to eat normal dog food, preferring to eat rats instead.

DNA testing solved the mystery. Turns out the animal was a cross between a stray dog and a pampas fox, a kind of ***false fox*** that inhabits Brazil's grassy plains. It was the first documented case of a dog-fox hybrid.

Scientists named the newly discovered species dogxim, which is a cross between *dog* and *graxaim-do-campo*, the Portuguese name for pampas fox.

As Brazil's wilderness shrinks to make room for houses, factories and roads, pampas and other foxes are forced to live near human settlements, which increases the chance of dog-fox interbreeding. Doxes, fogs and dogxim just might be the canine wave of the future!

AGUSTAVOP/GETTY IMAGES

The problem with mules, though, is that they can't produce offspring. It's because the mule's horse and donkey parents do not have the same number of ***chromosomes***, those chemical blueprints strung together in every strand of DNA. Chromosomes contain the genes that, collectively, determine an organism's traits. Every species has a specific number of chromosomes. Closely related species have the same number of chromosomes. Dogs and wolves, for example, have 78. But donkeys have 62 chromosomes, and horses 64. That leaves mules with 63 chromosomes, an uneven pairing that makes them ***infertile*** and increases their chance of having health problems.

ANCIENT VERSUS MODERN

In any case, given the genetic similarities and the fact that wolf-dog puppies could successfully mate, it's no wonder scientists believed they were the same species. But a 2020 study led by the Frances Crick Institute in London, one of the world's leading genetic research organizations, challenged this theory. Researchers compared 100,000 years of wolf DNA with genes from modern dogs and discovered something that surprised everyone. Turns out, today's dogs are more closely related to ancient wolves than to modern ones. This means that dogs were not a domesticated gray wolf, but rather that both wolves and dogs shared a common ancestor.

As to how these ancient wolves evolved into the two species we know today, no one knows for sure.

What we do know is that at some point during the last Ice Age, two different species began to emerge. Maybe a group of them got isolated and over time adapted to their unique environment. It's possible, for example, that the future wolves evolved in a place where meat was plentiful, and humans were few and far between. This could explain why they became carnivorous hunters wary of human contact. These future dogs, on the other hand, might have evolved in a place where meat was scarce and human contact was unavoidable—or maybe even essential—to their survival as a species. No matter how it happened, the results are undisputable. Dogs and wolves have gone their separate ways, while dogs and people forged a friendship that has lasted thousands of years.

KISSING (CANINE) COUSINS

Which modern dog breeds are most closely related to gray wolves? You might not be surprised to learn that huskies and malamutes have more DNA in common with gray wolves than any other dog breeds. Both breeds look pretty wolflike and share traits such as a thick undercoat (for those cold northern winters), powerful bodies and a keen sense of smell.

The next closest relatives? Well, here's where things get weird. It turns out that shih tzus and Pekingese, tiny lapdogs originally from China that look nothing like wolves, share more DNA with gray wolves than almost any other breed besides huskies and malamutes.

The main reason they are so wolflike? The shih tzu and Pekingese breeds are both very old, and the dogs lived in relative isolation for a long time. They didn't have a chance to mix and mate with other kinds of dogs. The result is a close DNA match to the gray wolf.

Dogs and gray wolves share 99 percent of their DNA... and a common ancestor.
ANTONIO_DIAZ/GETTY IMAGES

A boy and his dog out for a walk.
SAWITREELYAON/GETTY IMAGES

4

DAWN OF THE DOG

Once upon a time, a boy took his dog for a walk. It wasn't an ordinary stroll through the park, though. The boy wanted an adventure. He'd heard about a cave hidden in the mountains near his home. He wanted to go explore it. So the boy and his dog set off.

They hiked up a steep trail until they came to a narrow crack in the limestone. They quickly squeezed through it, and next thing they knew, they were standing in a vast underground cavern spiked with bone-white stalactites and stalagmites. The boy lifted his torch to get a better look. It was hard to make out anything in the flickering shadows, but he noticed something interesting on the wall just ahead. The two moved a little closer, and the image became clearer. It was a drawing of a horse's head by an artist so skilled, the picture almost looked real.

A detail from the replica of the Chauvet Cave and the 30,000-year-old paintings found on the walls of the original cave.
BRUNO M PHOTOGRAPHIE/ SHUTTERSTOCK.COM

The boy shifted his torch. Over there, a drawing of a cave bear. Next to that, a herd of reindeer…

The companions explored the cave for almost an hour, discovering dozens of paintings of cave lions and mammoths, woolly rhinoceroses and bison, red deer, ibexes and aurochs (an ancient ancestor of the cow). After a while they left, went home and no doubt told their friends and family about the discovery.

It's a nice little story that seems quite ordinary until you realize it happened 25,000 years ago. Not only that, but the paintings were already 5,000 years old when the boy and his dog discovered them.

A TIMELESS STORY ETCHED IN CLAY

How do we know about this ancient art-gallery visit? The secret lies on the cave floor. To explain, we need to go back to another young cave explorer. It was a sunny winter Sunday in the French village of Vallon-Pont-d'Arc when Jean-Marie Chauvet (pronounced SHOW-vay) decided to go exploring. He wanted to look for hidden caves in the nearby mountains. He heard about a newly discovered crack in the rocks. Was it a promising lead?

Chauvet set off with a couple of friends, and they soon found the crack. But what a disappointment it was! It didn't look like an entrance to anything, just a small hole in the limestone, barely the size of his fist. Chauvet peeked inside the hole. Nothing but darkness.

As he turned to go, a puff of moist air breezed across his face. Chauvet stopped. To an experienced cave hunter, a tiny wind means there could be a hidden cave below. The three friends began digging. Soon they'd made a hole big enough to crawl through, and one by one they squeezed through a narrow tunnel. They crawled 10 feet (3 meters) before coming to a sudden drop. Had their adventure stopped before it even started?

Chauvet turned on his flashlight and saw a vast cavern below. He and his friends could not believe their luck. As they lowered themselves into the cavern, Chauvet and his friends had no way of knowing that they had not only discovered a long-lost cave but had also stumbled into one of the most important ***archaeological*** sites the world had ever seen.

What secrets are hidden deep inside these rocks?

JYB DEVOT/WIKIMEDIA COMMONS/ CC BY-SA 4.0

TIMELINE OF ANIMAL DOMESTICATION

YEARS AGO	ANIMAL	LOCATION
15,000+	Dogs	Unknown
10,500	Sheep	Asia
10,000	Goats	Asia
9,000	Cats Pigs Cows	Middle East Asia Africa
8,000	Chickens	Asia
7,000	Guinea pigs (for food!) Zebu (humped cattle)	Peru India
6,500	Llamas, alpacas	Peru
6,000	Donkeys	Africa
4,000	Ducks Camels Bees	Asia Middle East Asia
5,500	Horses	Kazakhstan
5,000	Honeybees Yaks	Asia Tibet
4,500	Water buffalo	Pakistan
3,500	Geese	Europe
3,000	Reindeer	Siberia
2,000	Turkeys	Mexico

TIMOTHY ALLEN/GETTY IMAGES

ANCIENT FOOTPRINTS WITH A STORY TO TELL

What's so special about Chauvet Cave (as it's come to be called)? Turns out, the walls and ceiling are covered in more than 1,000 paintings, dating back 36,000 years. It's some of the earliest artwork ever discovered.

The cave held another, equally important surprise for scientists. Two sets of footprints were left behind in the clay. One set belongs to a human, the other to some kind of dog. Turns out that when our Paleolithic boy and his prehistoric canine pal went for a wander through the cave 25,000 years earlier, they literally left their mark in the damp clay floor. Archaeologists have carefully examined the ancient prints, piecing together the pair's ancient tour of this gallery in stunning detail.

Can you make out the 25,000-year-old prints of the boy and his dog?

ALEXIS ORAND/GETTY IMAGES

SIDE BY SIDE

Based on the size and shape of the human prints, scientists can tell they were made by a boy nine or ten years old and roughly 4.5 feet (1.5 meters) tall. The spacing and angle of the footprints tell us the boy walked slowly for 150 feet (45 meters) through the dark chamber. There's a smudged print at one point where the boy slipped. Farther on, where the cave narrows, there is still a charcoal stain on the ceiling from the boy's torch. This is where he and the dog stopped to take a rest.

The dog's prints have their own tale to tell. The animal has a shortened middle digit on the front paw, a clear sign that it is not a wolf. Only dogs have a paw print like this. The angle of the prints also tells us that the dog wasn't hunched down but was walking on all fours and matching the boy's pace step for step.

PŘEDMOSTÍ'S PALEO POOCH

Researchers at Předmostí, in the Czech Republic, recently uncovered the remains of three odd-looking dogs. The animals were wolflike but were smaller and more compact and had shorter snouts than modern wolves. Yet the skeletons also had some doglike qualities. In particular, the skulls looked similar to those of modern-day huskies. Were they dogs or wolves? No one was sure.

One thing was certain: these canines had lived with humans. Their 31,000-year-old fossils were found at a site littered with hundreds of human bones, and the brains had been carefully extracted from all three skulls. Was it part of a ritual to prepare the animals for their journey through the afterlife?

The biggest surprise was that one of the skulls had a mammoth bone wedged between its teeth. Clearly, the bone had been put there by a human. Was it a joke or another part of a spiritual ritual? The final verdict was that these were Paleolithic dogs, a close relative of the wolf and a direct ancestor of modern dogs that lived 15,000 to 40,000 years ago.

HOUNDS OF THE STONE AGE

Paleolithic dogs are the predecessor of the modern dog, but they're not directly descended from wolves. Instead, the two species have an ancient wolf ancestor in common.

Paleolithic dogs looked kind of like a wolf but had their own unique traits. They were smaller and less bulky than wolves. Their ears were smaller, too, and not as pointy, while their tails drooped a little, unlike the wolf's firm, upright tail. Their fur was probably shaggier and softer than a wolf's, but still thick enough to keep the animal warm through those endless winter nights. As to the color? No one knows for sure but it was probably a mix of gray and brown, to allow them to blend in with their surroundings.

As to what ultimately happened to these Stone Age dogs, that's less of a mystery. They didn't become extinct. They just evolved over time to live with humans to and then, eventually, become the loving pet we know today.

GAS-PHOTO/SHUTTERSTOCK.COM

One thing's for sure: the pawprints found in Chauvet Cave were big.
DOUG DEMAREST/DESIGN PICS/ GETTY IMAGES

In other words, this wasn't a dangerous predator secretly stalking its prey. It was a trusted companion walking side by side with its friend as together they explored the cave's wonders.

DISCOVERY TURNS THE WORLD ON ITS HEAD

The prints caused an uproar in the scientific community and called theories of dog domestication into question. Before Chauvet Cave, most scientists thought that dogs had been domesticated 10,000 to 12,000 years ago. But these markings were 25,000 years old. How could that be possible?

BARKING UP THE FAMILY TREE

If the extended dog family ever has a reunion, it's going to be crowded. There are more than 35 types of canines, including:

- **DOGS:** One species (360+ recognized breeds).
- **WOLVES:** Three species (gray, red and Eastern) and 40 subspecies.
- **DINGOES:** Australia's native canines were declared a separate species in 2014. Related to dogs and wolves (dingoes can breed with both species), there are three subspecies: desert, alpine and northern.

- **COYOTES:** One species, 19 subspecies, all unique to North and Central America.
- **FOXES:** Twelve species, including the famous red and arctic foxes, and the ridiculously cute fennec fox.
- **FALSE FOXES:** Ten species of "false foxes," a canine that looks like a fox but is closer genetically to dogs and wolves. Six of the false fox species are native to South America, including Andean, Darwin's and pampas foxes.
- **JACKALS:** Found in parts of Europe and Africa, and throughout Asia. The four species are the golden, side-striped and black-backed jackals, and the African golden wolf.

- **RACCOON DOGS:** Maybe the cutest canine of all, and there are two subspecies: the common raccoon dog (found in Siberia, China, Vietnam and Korea) and the Japanese raccoon dog (native to, you guessed it, Japan). Related to foxes, they have racoon-like markings on their faces, squat bodies and bulky tails. They are not at all related to raccoons.

(TOP) JASON EDWARDS/GETTY IMAGES; (MIDDLE) DAVID C STEPHENS/GETTY IMAGES; (BOTTOM) JURGEN SCHMIDT/GETTY IMAGES

Maybe it wasn't a real dog, some argued. It could have been a wolf with a wonky paw. But most scientists realized that the discovery was a game changer. Before Chauvet Cave, scientists had thought humans deliberately domesticated dogs for purely practical reasons—dogs helped us in the hunt, guarded our flocks and watched over us as we slept. But here was evidence of two companions on a leisurely stroll, exploring a cave together. This was not a master leading his beast—it was two friends walking together, enjoying each other's company.

The curious prints got scientists thinking. Was it possible that domestication wasn't a one-way process of humans taming wild canines? Was it maybe a cooperative and mutually beneficial process, with both dogs and humans getting something out of it? Who knows? Maybe humans didn't domesticate dogs at all. Maybe they domesticated us.

Maybe dogs domesticated us, not the other way around.
DANIELA DUNCAN/GETTY IMAGES

No one knows exactly where ancestors of the modern dog came from.
DANIELA DUNCAN/GETTY IMAGES

5

WHERE ON EARTH?

Where did dogs originate? It's a question that scientists are still trying to answer. Not so long ago, people believed in something called the single-origin theory, which maintained that dogs were domesticated only once and in a specific part of the world. As to where this place was, no one could agree. Some said the Middle East, places like Iran, Iraq, Israel and Jordan. Twelve-thousand-year-old dog bones found at archaeological sites such as Shuqba Cave in Israel and Ganj Dareh in Iran give credence to the idea of a Middle Eastern origin.

East Asia was also another possibility. The DNA from modern dogs across Nepal, India and Mongolia indicates the breeds are closely related and have changed very little over time. One breed, the tazy, was even kind of a prehistoric viral sensation—the dogs' image can be

OLDEST SPECIES IN THE WORLD

BASENJI: Originating in Central Africa, specifically the Congo region, the basenji is one of the oldest known dog breeds, dating back to ancient Egypt around 6000 BCE. Basenjis are known for not being able to bark. They vocalize using a distinctive yodeling sound.

- **SALUKI:** An ancient breed believed to have originated in the Middle East about 8,000 to 9,000 years ago. Prized by the ancient Egyptians, salukis were often depicted in tombs and artifacts, symbolizing nobility and grace.

SIBERIAN HUSKY: One of the oldest sled-dog breeds, these dogs are believed to have originated thousands of years ago in Siberia. Renowned for their endurance, strength and thick double coat, Siberian huskies are used by the Chukchi people for transportation and companionship.

SHAR-PEI: An ancient breed originating from China, with origins dating back to around 200 BCE. Known for their distinctive wrinkled skin and "hippopotamus" muzzle shape, shar-peis were originally bred for tasks including hunting, herding and guarding.

- **TIBETAN MASTIFF:** Originating in the Himalayan Mountains, mastiffs have been around for thousands of years. Because of their imposing size and protective instincts, mastiffs were originally bred by monks to protect their livestock from wolves and other predators.

PEKINGESE: Another ancient breed originating from China, with a history dating back more than 2,000 years. Selectively bred to resemble tiny lions, which are revered in Chinese culture, Pekingese were favored by royalty as cherished companions.

(TOP LEFT) OMICOM/WIKIMEDIA COMMONS/PUBLIC DOMAIN; (TOP RIGHT) JOHN MCKEEN/GETTY IMAGES; (BOTTOM) DEVIDDO/GETTY IMAGES

found in hundreds of 3,000-year-old petroglyphs scattered across the mountains of southern Kazakhstan.

China was also in the mix. There's evidence that ancient Chinese breeds like chow chows have been around for more than 8,000 years. Europe too was a possibility. A fossilized jawbone discovered in a cave in northern Spain in 1986 dates back some 17,000 years, making it, at the time, the oldest confirmed dog bone ever found.

Dogs might have originated somewhere in East Asia. This street dog relaxes outside the Swayambhunath temple in Nepal.
GERAINT ROWLAND PHOTOGRAPHY/ GETTY IMAGES

RECORD-SETTING DISCOVERIES

That record seems to have fallen, though. Russian archaeologists have found a 33,000-year-old canine skull in a cave in the Altai Mountains of Central Asia. Meanwhile, researchers in Belgium have discovered three ancient skulls of roughly the same age. These fossils all show traits found in both dogs and wolves, so no one is sure what scientists are dealing with. Is it a kind of early dog? Semi-domesticated wolf? A wolf-dog hybrid? The testing continues.

On the surface, the single-origin theory makes sense. Despite the physical differences between dog breeds (think of the giant Saint Bernard versus the tiny Chihuahua), all dogs are biologically the same. It makes sense that they all would have come from the same place, right?

Some records say that dogs originated in Central Asia.
ANTONIO_DIAZ/ GETTY IMAGES

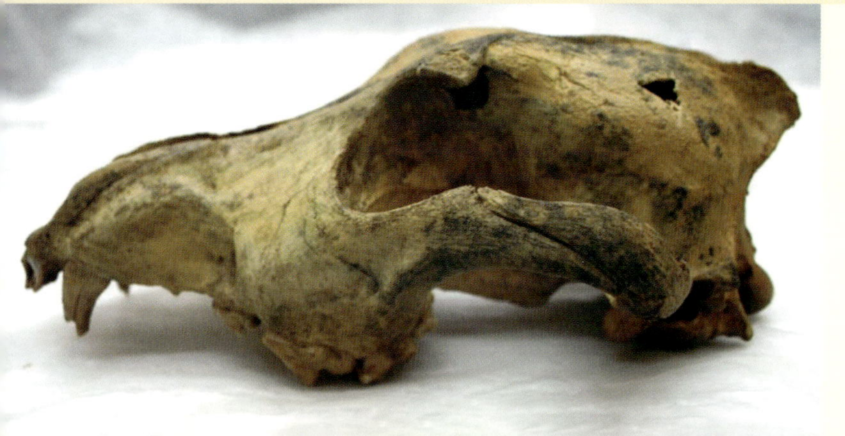

This 33,500-year-old dog skull from Central Asia might be one of the oldest ever found.
N. OVODOV, S. CROCKFORD ET AL./ WIKIMEDIA COMMONS/CC BY 2.5

Well...maybe not. In 2016 a study by researchers at Oxford University compared the DNA of 59 ancient dogs from all over Europe and Asia, then compared those results to the DNA of 2,500 modern dogs. The results amazed everyone. Turns out there's a clear genetic difference between the dogs from Asia and the ones from Europe. This means that the two groups evolved independently of each other.

AND THEN THERE WERE TWO

Enter the two-origins theory, which was built on the idea of two geographically distinct groups of dogs developing separately at roughly the same time. About 4,500 years ago, some curious things happened that seemed to have nothing to do with dogs. Interest in exotic spices started to grow. Spices like ginger, clove and nutmeg became hugely popular in Europe. Because these spices were only available in the Middle East and Asia, their value skyrocketed. It's hard to imagine now, but cinnamon became so popular, it was worth more than gold.

A prosperous international spice trade developed, with businesspeople from the East bringing their goods westward to sell in Europe. Of course, wherever people went, their dogs followed. These Eastern dogs mated with the Western breeds, and in time (and for reasons no one fully understands yet), the Asian dogs thrived and began to dominate the ***gene pool***. The result? Most of today's dogs are descendants of Asian—not European—dogs.

The tazy is an ancient breed from Kazakhstan.

NATALLIA YAUMENENKA/ SHUTTERSTOCK.COM

TWO ORIGINS ARE BETTER THAN ONE

Many people found the two-origins theory hard to accept. How could two groups of ancient peoples, who had no contact with one another, domesticate dogs at exactly the same time? It seemed like an improbable coincidence. But remember, when the two-origins theory came out, most people believed that dogs were directly descended from wolves. The idea that a group of people managed to tame the notoriously wild and wary wolf was hard enough to believe. But two separate groups doing it at the same time? That was a stretch.

But now, as more scientists see dogs and wolves as separate species, the two-origins theory is easier to accept. Dogs, after all, were genetically inclined to domestication. So the fact it happened in two places at once is not so hard to believe after all.

TAZY

The tazy, also known as the Kazakh greyhound, is a remarkable breed with a rich history that dates back thousands of years. Originally from the steppes of Central Asia, tazies are elegant animals that have long been prized for their agility, speed and loyalty. Sleek and slender, they can run 25 miles (40 kilometers) per hour and were known as fierce hunters that could even take down a full-grown wolf.

Like greyhounds, whippets and other superfast dogs, tazies are sight hounds, which means they hunt using their keen vision and tremendous speed. Even though they've been around for thousands of years, tazies are rarely found outside Central Asia. They remain relatively unchanged since prehistoric times.

DOGS: USER-FRIENDLY WOLVES

The earliest dogs already had inherited traits that made them more human-friendly than their wolf cousins. Thanks to their unique DNA, ancient dogs were, by nature, less aggressive and more open to new experiences. They were also less wary of new situations, which meant it was easier for them to interact with humans and other strange canines.

As we learned earlier, dogs have to be experts in reading human facial expressions and body language. And just as dogs have evolved to better engage with humans, humans have also undergone genetic changes that make us perfectly suited to connect with our furry friends. Like dogs, we've developed unique vocalizations, facial expressions and body language that dogs can understand and respond to. For example, when we speak to dogs in a high-pitched, friendly tone, they are more likely to approach us and show affection. This ability to communicate effectively strengthens the bond between humans and dogs and enhances our ability to work together as companions.

The ability to communicate strengthens the bond between dogs and their people.
SHAW PHOTOGRAPHY CO./GETTY IMAGES

DOGS ON THE BRAIN

It's not just our communication skills that have evolved to accommodate our canine friends. Studies have shown that humans have genetic variations associated with empathy and social bonding, which make us more inclined to care for and connect with animals, including dogs. These genetic predispositions drive us

Love hormones help bond you to your dog.
FOTOGRAFIXX/ GETTY IMAGES

to seek out the company of dogs, form strong attachments to them and take care of them.

Why did we evolve this way? Scientists are still trying to figure out the answer. But it may have something to do with how humans care for their own offspring. Because of our big brains, it takes a long time for humans to grow into independent adults. So we evolved strong nurturing and bonding instincts. It's possible that dogs accidentally found a place in our hearts by evolving in a way that takes advantage of our child-rearing instincts.

Perhaps most remarkable of all, both of us—dogs and humans—have undergone chemical changes. You know when you look into your dog's eyes and feel warm all over? Well, your dog feels it too. It's because both of you produce higher levels of a brain chemical called oxytocin. A dose of this chemical, also known as the love hormone, leaves us feeling calm and literally warm all over. It's a chemical connection that bonds you to your four-legged BFF.

A WORD ABOUT CATS

The relationship between humans and cats goes back 10,000 years or more. All modern house cats are descended from the Near Eastern wildcat, which still roams the deserts of Israel, Egypt, Saudi Arabia and other Middle Eastern countries. These cats look a lot like the tabby cats of today.

The Near Eastern wildcats were smaller and less wary of humans than other wildcats, which made them a good candidate for domestication. They also have a taste for mice, rats and other small rodents, which is probably what got them mixed up with humans in the first place.

Back in the day when humans moved from being hunter-gatherers to farmers, we started building storehouses to keep our grain dry and safe. Mice love grain, cats love mice...and the rest is history.

JESUSHERRERA/SHUTTERSTOCK.COM

Dogs come in all sizes, shapes, colors and attitudes.
STEFAN CRISTIAN CIOATA/GETTY IMAGES

ONE GOOD BREED DESERVES ANOTHER

Look around. On the sidewalks and in parks and backyards, a world of dogs. From diminutive dachshunds to the great big Great Danes, dogs come in an array of sizes, shapes, colors and attitudes. There are hundreds of *different dog breeds*...and more are being added to the list all the time.

What exactly is a breed? For starters, it's different from a species, which is the basic biological classification that groups closely related plants and animals together. Breeds are a subgroup within a species. For instance, all domestic dogs belong to the species *Canis lupus familiaris*. Smaller groups within a species, like Labrador retrievers and German shepherds, are called breeds.

STRANGE STARTS

BRITISH BULLDOGS: These powerful, pug-faced pooches were bred to fight and subdue bulls in an unpleasant ancient sport called bull baiting.

CHIHUAHUAS: This itsy-bitsy dog was originally bred for multiple jobs, including ratcatcher, food source (yup, people used to eat them) and bed warmer.

DACHSHUNDS: With their short legs and narrow bodies, dachshunds were built to crawl into badger burrows and fox holes and help farmers chase away these unwanted animals.

GREAT DANES: Bred to hunt boars (basically, wild pigs), Great Danes are powerful, aggressive hunters but gentle human companions.

POMERANIANS: Don't let these little powder puffs fool you. Queen Victoria's favorite breed packs a lot of punch. Named after a region in Poland where they used to be popular, Pomeranians were originally bred to be sled dogs.

PUGS: First bred in ancient China, cute and cuddly pugs are one of the few ancient breeds specifically designed to be lap dogs.

SAINT BERNARDS: Now famous as a rescue dog, Saint Bernards were designed for life in the high mountains, where they could use their big bodies to plow walking paths through the snow.

WELSH CORGIS: Hard to believe, but these waddling little cuties were originally bred to herd cattle. It seems an odd job until you realize their low, narrow bodies allow them to nip at a cow's ankle to get it to go in the right direction.

Every breed has a story to tell.
DANIELA DUNCAN/GETTY IMAGES

But where did breeds come from? Well, once upon a time most dogs looked similar (the way wolves today all look similar). People noticed, though, that some dogs were better at certain things. Some could run fast. Some were good at chasing rats. Some had a super sense of smell. So people started breeding dogs selectively, matching a great herder or super sniffer with a similarly gifted mate. The chance that their offspring would also share this trait was high.

Over thousands of years, humans became good at creating breeds that could help with very specific tasks. Labrador retrievers, for example, were bred to help fishers retrieve fish. Their thick, water-resistant coats and webbed feet made them excellent swimmers, while their friendly nature and intelligence made them the perfect helpmates.

GENES TO THE RESCUE

How does selective breeding work? Remember our old friend the gene? Genes are the strands of chemical information inside your DNA that help determine your physical and personality traits. Your genes (all 20,000 to 25,000 of them) come in pairs, with one gene inherited from your mom, the other from your dad. Together these pairs add up to give you specific traits—height, eye color, hairy knuckles.

Some dogs, like Labrador retrievers, were bred to be great swimmers.

NOEL HENDRICKSON/GETTY IMAGES

THE EYES HAVE IT

Is there more to a dog than meets the eyes? According to researchers at Japan's Teikyo University of Science, there's a lot of evolutionary history in a dog's eye color. Specifically, the researchers wanted to know if there was a significant difference between wolf and dog eye color. They compared the irises of 22 gray wolves and dogs from 35 different breeds. Their findings? Dogs tended to have brown eyes (or, to a lesser extent, blue), while wolves tended toward yellow. The researchers also tested how people reacted to the different eye colors and discovered that most found the darker eyes friendlier. It's another example of how dogs and people have coevolved to ensure that our mutual bond is strong.

Some genes are dominant, which means they influence a trait more than a recessive gene does. It doesn't matter which parent you get the gene from. If one gene is dominant, it will have a stronger influence on the trait.

Take eye color, for example. In humans, the gene for brown eyes is dominant while the gene for blue eyes is recessive. So if you have one brown-eye gene and one blue-eye gene, you're likely going to have brown eyes. Green eye color is interesting, though. It's a mix of both—green is dominant to blue but recessive to brown.

ARCTIC NIGHTS

When it comes to dogs, the basic gene rules are the same, which is why most of them (more than 80 percent of them) have brown eyes. But there are some curious exceptions. Think of the Siberian husky with its striking steel-blue eyes. The breed is prone to a genetic mutation that makes blue eyes dominant. It might be an evolutionary adaptation, since this eye color helps dogs see better in the dark—an advantage during those six-month-long Arctic nights.

The striking blue eyes of a Siberian husky.
8213ERIKA/GETTY IMAGES

Huskies are one of the oldest breeds around.
KALI9/GETTY IMAGES

Of course, our ancient ancestors didn't know the ins and outs of genetics. But they were keen observers and couldn't help but notice that with a little timely matchmaking, they could give Mother Nature a helping hand. Once again, huskies are a good example. Originally from Siberia—and one of the oldest surviving breeds on Earth—huskies no doubt started as a hardy breed already adapted to the extreme northern climate.

DAVID HERLIANTO/SHUTTERSTOCK.COM

THE ANCIENT CAANAN DOG

Caanan dogs were one of the first herding dogs humans ever bred. Originally from Canaan, an ancient area that included parts of Israel, Palestine, Lebanon and Syria, the dogs were an important part of the lives of the nomadic Bedouin people.

Unfortunately, the number of Canaan dogs has been declining for the last hundred years. One of the main reasons is due to the fact that they tend to live outdoors rather than in homes with humans. This makes it easier for them to get rabies, a serious disease that dogs catch from other animals and, in turn, can pass on to humans. Humans can catch rabies from a dog bite or even by being licked by an infected dog. While the disease is easy to treat in its early stages, it is almost always fatal if untreated. So the government caught and destroyed these dogs to protect public health.

Thankfully people in the area have started to see that ancient dogs are an important part of their history and heritage. Efforts continue to protect these amazing animals. While they may no longer roam the deserts of Canaan in the same numbers, they are now a sought-after breed popular around the world.

BREEDS, BREEDS, BREEDS

The process of selective breeding accelerated during the Middle Ages (500 to 1500) with the rise of feudal societies and the development of specialized roles for dogs. Nobles and royalty began breeding dogs for specific purposes, such as hunting, guarding and companionship. This led to the creation of breeds like the greyhound, which was prized for its speed and agility in chasing down game, and the mastiff, which was valued for its size and strength as a guardian and protector.

The concept of dog breeds as we know them today really began to take shape in the United Kingdom during the Victorian era. It was a time when the country was obsessed

In the Middle Ages, nobles bred dogs for the hunt.
GRAFISSIMO/GETTY IMAGES

with discovery, invention and innovation. People at the time brought this attitude to dogs and were always looking to create a new breed that could help people work more effectively.

It was also a time when the idea of pets first began to take shape. As the middle class grew and more people had extra money to spend, dogs became popular as both companions and status symbols. The idea was that if you could afford to spend money on something as "useless" as a nonworking animal, you must be successful. To go along with dogs' newly found status, things like kennel clubs and ***breed standards*** became popular as a way of enhancing a dog's prestige. If your dog had the right bloodlines, it made your pet seem special, like an animal aristocrat.

The era gave us some of our most-loved dog breeds. German shepherds, beagles, Irish setters, dachshunds, Labrador retrievers—all of these were created by the innovative breeders of the Victorian era.

Dogs as pets became popular during the Victorian era.
ILBUSCA/GETTY IMAGES

VICTORIA AND DASH

The Victorian era was named after the queen who ruled the United Kingdom at the time. Victoria was on the throne from June 20, 1837, to January 22, 1901. Even though she was a princess, Victoria had a sad childhood. Her parents were too busy to pay her much attention. Isolated from other kids, she didn't have any friends.

On her 13th birthday her parents gave her a special gift: a spaniel she named Dash. Dash became Victoria's only friend and started her lifelong love affair with dogs. Victoria owned dozens of dogs in her life and was particularly fond of Pomeranians. Victoria even bred her own Poms, helping make the dog popular across Europe.

Victoria's love of dogs never diminished. As she lay on her deathbed, one of her final requests was for someone to get Turi, her favorite Pomeranian, and lay him by her side.

ROYAL COLLECTION/WIKIMEDIA COMMONS/ PUBLIC DOMAIN

A Peruvian hairless dog.
GUSTAVO RAMIREZ/GETTY IMAGES

THE AMERICAS GO TO THE DOGS

If you visit Huaca Pucllana, an ancient pyramid in the middle of Lima, Peru, you'll find some of the strangest-looking dogs on Earth. Mostly bald, with leathered, warty skin and and often with a tuft of orange hair on the top of their heads, they are the punk rockers of the dog world. They are also one of the most ancient breeds around. They are known by many names—moondog, Chimú, devil dogs—although in Peru everyone calls them los perros sin pelo—the dogs without hair. These hairless dogs are an important part of the history and culture of this South American country. Centuries ago, the Inca used the animals for hunting, protecting their crops and herding llamas and alpacas. They even welcomed the dogs into their beds—these naked pooches made perfect bed warmers on long, cold nights.

GONE AND ALMOST FORGOTTEN

Here are just of the few of the more than 70 dog species you would have encountered in the Americas 500 years ago. They are all extinct now.

- **AON:** When explorer Christopher Columbus reached the Caribbean, he encountered an interesting dog breed kept by the Taino People. The dog was roughly the same size and shape as a Chihuahua and, according to Columbus, didn't bark but instead "whistled, chortled and howled."
- **CHIRIBAYA:** A small dog bred by the Indigenous People of Peru. The dog was used for hunting and herding, and it was an important part of the culture of the Chiribaya people.
- **FUEGIAN:** Native to the southern tip of South America, particularly Tierra del Fuego, these were companion dogs who helped with the hunt. They looked a lot like foxes, and for a long time scientists included them in the fox family.
- **COAST SALISH WOOLLY DOG:** Found in the Haida Gwaii archipelago off the coast of British Columbia, the dogs were prized by the First Nations of the area for their dense, woolly coats, which, like sheep's wool, were used for making clothing and blankets.
- **HARE INDIAN DOG:** A small- to medium-sized breed connected to the Dene First Nations located in northern Canada. These dogs were valued for their hunting abilities, particularly in pursuing game such as hares and ptarmigans.
- **TAHLTAN BEAR DOG:** Bred by the Tahltan First Nation in northern British Columbia, the dogs were keen hunters and loving companions. They were fearless, too, and helped hunt bears and other large game.

(TOP) UNKNOWN AUTHOR/WIKIMEDIA COMMONS/PUBLIC DOMAIN; (BOTTOM) ALEXANDER MIRT/DREAMSTIME.COM

WORLD TRAVELERS

History hasn't always been kind to los perros sin pelo. But the dogs' origins tell us a lot about the history of dog domestication. The breed's story begins thousands of years ago with a great adventure from one continent to another. Toward the end of the last Ice Age, global sea levels were much lower. This resulted in the formation of a geological corridor, known as the Bering Land Bridge, that connected North America to Asia. Ancient hunter-gatherers from Asia crossed the corridor to the Americas 21,000 to 23,000 years ago.

They were among the first humans to set foot in the area. They ventured across the land bridge, following the herds of animals that roamed these frigid grasslands. Their journey was fraught with challenges, from extreme cold to treacherous terrain to vicious predators like saber-toothed cats, with razor-sharp fangs, and 12-foot (3.5-meter) tall prehistoric bears, the most dangerous mammal in the Americas at the time.

Yet these people's determination to seek new opportunities, resources and a better life for their families drove the nomads forward. And where they went, their dogs followed. Exactly what did these canines look like? DNA evidence suggests the dogs were direct ancestors of the modern-day huskies and malamutes. Originally from Siberia, these early sled dogs also gave us modern-day Mongolian and Siberian breeds like Samoyed, Chinook and Laika. The ancient dogs had thick coats, like huskies, not to mention the incredible strength and endurance required to pull sleds over long distances.

BERING LAND BRIDGE

Think back 20,000 years. A quarter of the planet was covered in glaciers, and the oceans' water levels dropped 400 feet (120 meters). This left an exposed corridor of land more than 600 miles (1,000 kilometers) long, stretching from Siberia to Alaska. Geologists call it the Bering Land Bridge.

As the climate warmed and glaciers melted, the rising oceans gradually submerged the land bridge. By the end of the last Ice Age, 11,000 years ago, the Americas were completely cut off from the rest of the world, and whole new civilizations, languages and dog breeds spread across the lands.

AMANDA LANIK, BECKER ET AL. (2009) AND EHLERS ET AL. (2011)/NPS

HAPPY WANDERERS

As humans spread across the Americas, so did their dogs, adapting to new environments along the way. Eventually the descendants of these first dogs could be found all over the Americas. Their populations remained stable for thousands of years, until the 15th century, when Europeans started coming to the Americas. Their arrival changed the land, the people and their dogs forever.

These newcomers caused tremendous upheaval for the Indigenous Peoples of the Americas. Before the arrival of Europeans, the Indigenous population was between 50 and 100 million. Disease, war and ***famine*** took their toll. Within 200 years, that population was less than than 7,000.

The effect on the dog population was just as catastrophic. Before Europeans arrived, there were more than 70 dog breeds in the Americas. Within 100 years, almost every one of those breeds was gone. Disease killed many of them. They had no resistance to infections brought over by European dogs.

The colonizers themselves did a lot of damage to dog populations. They considered the Indigenous dogs uncivilized because they often lived in free-roaming packs. The Europeans set out to destroy the local dogs, hunting them for sport and food. The combination of disease and persecution almost completely wiped out these dogs. Most dogs in the Americas today have very little DNA from those early, Indigenous dogs—1 to 3 percent. That's about the same amount of Neanderthal DNA you would find in the average human.

The first dogs in the Americas looked a lot like huskies.
THEPALMER/GETTY IMAGES

VIVA LOS PERROS!

Peru's hairless dogs survived the arrival of Europeans and their dogs—but just barely. The Spanish ***conquistadors*** were not fans of the strange naked dog. They called it the demon dog (in part because the animal's half-floppy ears resembled devil's horns) and tried to wipe the breed out. They used the dogs for target practice and, for fun, would unleash their vicious becerrillo—bull mastiffs bred for battle—on the helpless perros sin pelo.

Peru's Indigenous dogs were eventually banished to the beaches and jungles. Shunned, unprotected, they scavenged for food. Their numbers dwindled, and by 2000 there were only a couple hundred perros sin pelo left on Earth.

But then something unexpected and rather remarkable happened. Peruvians started to take a greater interest in Indigenous history and, along the way, realized that their hairless dogs were an important part of their culture and heritage.

Today the dog's population has recovered nicely. In 2001 the government declared the breed the National Dog of Peru, and today these once-demonized "devil" dogs are a familiar sight across the country and prized by dog owners around the world.

Peru's "devil dog."
ATRFPPAMO/GETTY IMAGES

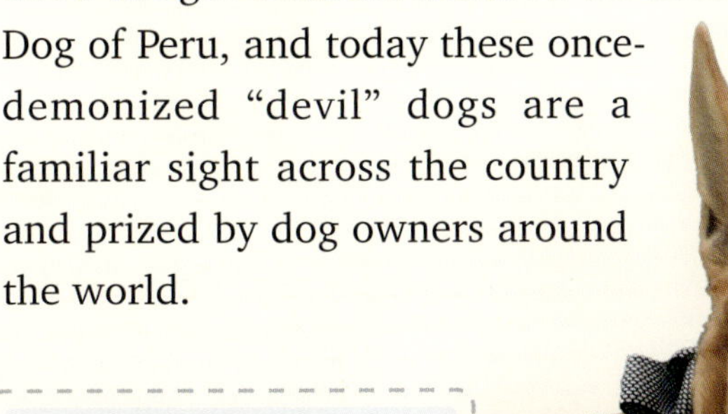

The Carolina dog, the only Indigenous dog in the United States outside of Alaska.
ANDREA VIELMA/GETTY IMAGES

THE AMERICAN DINGO

Meet the Carolina dog, which is very likely the only Indigenous dog in the United States (outside of Alaska). Also known as American dingoes because of their resemblance to Australia's famous wild dogs—they are not closely related—these dogs are true survivors. Believed to be descended from the Siberian dogs that followed early nomads across the Bering Land Bridge, these dogs were once found all over the southeastern United States. But colonizers shunned the dogs. They thought the animals were ***feral***—once-domesticated dogs that had gone wild. Banished to the forests and swamps, Carolina dogs were on the brink of extinction by the end of the 1800s.

Finally, in the 1950s, scientists discovered the dog's ancient lineage and efforts began to bring back the breed. Today—with programs in place to protect them—Carolina dogs are making a comeback.

What's next for dogs and people?
MINT IMAGES/GETTY IMAGES

8

A BIG, BRIGHT FUTURE WITH OUR BFFs

What does the future hold for humans and our four-pawed BFFs? Changing attitudes toward dog breeding, advances in technology and genetic science, and a new understanding of how dogs think and feel—all these trends could change the dog-human relationship. One major shift is in our attitude toward dog breeds. In the past, people thought ***purebreds*** were better than other dogs. Classic breeds like Labrador retrievers and French bulldogs are maintained by selectively mating dogs within one breed. But this ***inbreeding*** (the practice of mating closely related dogs) limits the genetic diversity of a breed and can have serious health consequences.

Because of inbreeding, black Labs, like my BFF Elvis, are susceptible to hip dysplasia—a potentially crippling medical disorder—and eye diseases that can lead to blindness.

PANDEMIC PUPPY CRAZE

During the COVID-19 pandemic, people turned to their BFFs for comfort and companionship. According to the American Pet Products Association, an estimated 11.38 million households in the United States acquired a new pet during the pandemic, with dogs being (by far) the most popular choice.

At the height of the pandemic, the American Society for the Prevention of Cruelty to Animals reported a 70 percent increase in foster applications, while doggy adoption rates doubled. Similarly, the Royal Society for the Prevention of Cruelty to Animals in the United Kingdom reported a 600 percent increase in adoption inquiries for dogs during the lockdown. Unfortunately, after the pandemic ended, a lot of these dogs were returned to shelters or abandoned.

Likewise Frenchies, with their distinctive flat noses and stunted jaws, often have breathing issues and spinal problems.

MIXED BREEDS AND RESCUES

As people better understand the risks of inbreeding, there's a growing understanding among dog owners of the health risks associated with purebred dogs. That means dog owners are moving away from purebred dogs toward mixed breeds.

Not long ago, mixed-breed dogs were shunned as inferior mutts. But attitudes have changed. Truth is, there's absolutely nothing wrong with mixed-breed dogs. In fact, because they have greater genetic diversity, they tend to have fewer health problems than purebreds. This change in attitude has opened the dog world up to whole new breeds. For example, breeders have mixed black Labs with border collies to create boradors—a breed that combines

Mixed breeds have fewer inherited health problems than purebreds.
LSOPHOTO/GETTY IMAGES

the Lab's friendly nature with the herding instincts of the collie. And don't forget Labradoodles, one of the most popular dogs around these days. A cross between Labs and standard poodles, these curly-haired dogs are friendly and intelligent, and they don't shed a lot—a bonus for people who have allergies or just want to keep their home cleaner.

Rescue dogs, as the name implies, have been saved from abandonment or mistreatment. They can be mixed breeds or purebreds. Many special organizations have sprung up to help find these dogs safe, stable homes. Most are put in foster homes until those forever homes are found, while others remain in shelters until they are adopted.

By embracing mixed-breed and rescues, we're not only putting dogs' health first, but we're also helping ensure the genetic diversity of the species. It's a positive shift that shows a more compassionate approach to caring for our forever friends.

Rescue dogs are being trained for their new homes.
SOLSTOCK/GETTY IMAGES

Get ready for robot dogs!
GORODENKOFF/GETTY IMAGES

Technology can help dogs that have been seriously injured.
ELENA POPOVA/GETTY IMAGES

HIGH-TECH HOUNDS

Technological advances also are helping ensure an exciting future for the dog-human partnership. Researchers are coming up with innovative tools and gadgets that make our BFFs an even bigger part of our lives. These innovations include:

ERIK ISAKSON/GETTY IMAGES

SMART COLLARS.

Rescue workers already use specially designed dog collars equipped with cameras and GPS tracking to find missing people. Handlers send dogs with smart collars into caves, collapsed buildings and other tight places where people can't fit, and the collars send back helpful information to the waiting rescuers. Dogs wearing smart collars are also sent into forests at night to use their keen sense of smell and night vision to find lost hikers.

COMPUTER-ASSISTED CANINES.

Service dogs are already being trained to support seniors and other-abled people by operating appliances and doing other household tasks. Now scientists are looking at ways to use computer technology to make homebound hounds even more helpful. One innovation from the Georgia Institute of Technology is a special doggy vest with a built-in computer chip that monitors the owner's health and safety. If there's a problem, the dog can trigger an alarm in its teeth that plays a recorded message telling other people the owner is in trouble.

GENETIC ENGINEERING.

Meanwhile, advances in genetic science and technology are unlocking the mysteries of dog-human coevolution. Someday—soon—questions about where, when and how dogs were domesticated will all be answered thanks to DNA research. This information will also help us make more informed decisions when it comes to how we breed dogs. Inherited disease due to inbreeding could someday be eliminated, while ***genetic engineering*** could introduce completely new traits into existing breeds. Can you imagine a dog that glows in the dark so drivers can better see them at night? Scientists are already working on it!

CHAT DOG.

Advances in artificial intelligence are also revolutionizing the way we communicate with our canine companions. Researchers are exploring ways that AI could help translate dog vocalizations and body language into human words. It's still early days, but imagine a day in the future when Google Translate includes a dog option.

SEBASTIAN KAULITZKI/SCIENCE PHOTO LIBRARY/GETTY IMAGES

GLOW DOGS, GLOW!

In a groundbreaking experiment, scientists in South Korea genetically modified beagle puppies to make them fluorescent. They achieved this remarkable feat by inserting the gene that makes creatures like fireflies and jellyfish glow into a puppy's DNA.

The scientists weren't just fooling around. The glow-in-the-dark genes were a way of helping them mark disease-causing DNA, in order to make it easier for them to follow the progress of a disease and—hopefully—find better ways to cure it. Since dogs and humans share 268 different diseases, the cutting-edge technology of ***gene editing*** might someday help make the world a healthier place for both dogs and humans. While the idea of genetically engineered glowing dogs may seem futuristic and even a little bit strange, it highlights the potential of technology in medical research.

SMARTER THAN WE EVER IMAGINED

Dogs are becoming more integrated into our communities and workplaces. Many companies allow dogs on site. Even schools are getting into the act, bringing in specially trained therapy dogs to help comfort students when the stress of studying gets to be too much.

This new attitude toward dogs is being driven by scientific research that's revealed the amazing emotional and intellectual power inside out BFFs' furry little heads.

We already talked about dogs and their amazing ability to understand human emotions and intentions. As you learned, researchers have discovered that dogs are keen observers of our facial expressions and vocal cues and use these to understand our emotions. And they go one step further, using this information to respond to us in helpful ways—an empathic cuddle when we're feeling lonely, a curious turn of the head and kisses when we need some attention.

Research has also shed light on the remarkable problem-solving abilities of dogs. It turns out that dogs possess a unique form of social intelligence that allows them to learn and complete complex tasks simply by observing human cues. In one test, for example, dogs were able to infer the location of hidden food based on subtle human gestures (casual glances, slight hand movements), which shows just how well they can read us.

A specially-trained dog is ready to lead a search-and-rescue mission.
EGON69/GETTY IMAGES

Friends indeed! A guide dog helps out his visually impaired friend.

FOTOGRAFIXX/GETTY IMAGES

ON THE SAME WAVELENGTH

Scientists have also discovered that dogs can understand things from the perspectives of both humans and other dogs. Studies have shown that through simple observation dogs can anticipate what other dogs are going to do. In your local dog park, for example, your pet pays close attention to what other dogs are doing to figure out who's there to play and who just wants to be left alone. To animal researchers, that ability to read others' moods indicates that dogs have a very good understanding of social situations.

TAKING THINGS TOO FAR?

Talk about puppy love. On July 30, 2019, fans of a newsmagazine show in the United Kingdom tuned in to watch a woman named Elizabeth Hoad walk down the aisle with her six-year-old golden retriever, Logan. Why would anyone marry their pet, let alone on national TV? Hoad told the TV host that she'd almost given up looking for the perfect partner when she realized true love was sitting right in front of her, panting and drooling. Logan was perfect. Friendly, happy, loyal. She told her friends she was going to marry him. It started as a joke...and then Hoad took things (sort of) more seriously.

Hoad wasn't the first person to tie the knot with their pet pooch. A decade earlier, Wilhelmina Callaghan was browsing the internet when she came across a website called marryyourpet.com, which called itself "the pet and people wedding specialists." It sounded like a laugh, so Callaghan paid a hundred bucks and got hitched to her Yorkshire terrier, Henry. The next thing she knew, Callaghan was flooded with social media comments, mostly from people angry she'd married a mutt.

Doctors use CAT scan machines to get a better idea of how a dog's brain works.
OLIVER ROSSI/GETTY IMAGES

Meanwhile, a high-tech piece of medical equipment called a magnetic resonance imaging (MRI) machine, which can trace ***neurological*** activity, has shown that dogs and humans think and feel in similar ways. To do the tests, though, researchers at Emory University in Atlanta, Georgia, first had to train dogs to lie absolutely still. You see, MRI machines are very sensitive, so any movement can throw the test off. In previous tests, dogs had to be sedated. By teaching them to remain motionless, researchers finally got to see the brain waves of a fully awake dog. The results were striking. The dogs' brain patterns were remarkably similar to humans', suggesting that coevolution has left both our species on literally the same wavelength.

Scientific research continues to uncover the depth of the intelligence and emotional sensitivity of dogs. From their understanding of human emotions to their problem-solving skills and social cognition, dogs demonstrate a level of cognitive complexity rivaling that of many other species. As our understanding of the canine mind deepens, so too does our appreciation for the unique bond we share with dogs, our furry best friends forever.

VIOLETASTOIMENOVA/GETTY IMAGES

COMING TO A PET STORE NEAR YOU

Just for fun, let's see what might it be like if humans took the designer-dog craze to the next level. None of these dog breeds are real, but it's fun to imagine the kinds of wild and crazy creatures we might be able to create in the future.

- **SOLAR SETTERS:** Developed for sustainability-conscious families, these dogs are bred to thrive in off-grid living environments. With solar panels integrated into their coats, they harness sunlight to power small devices and even provide energy for their own activities.
- **ROBO RETRIEVERS:** Engineered for aquatic adventures, these dogs are skilled swimmers with webbed feet and waterproof coats. They excel in water rescue missions and enjoy accompanying their owners on boating and swimming excursions.
- **HOVER HOUNDS:** Designed for urban living, hover hounds have specialized electromagnetic pads on their paws, enabling them to hover above ground surfaces. This unique trait reduces wear and tear on their joints—although we'd still have to figure out how to handle doggy-doo dropping from the sky.
- **ECO TERRIERS:** Bred to have a reduced carbon paw print, with traits such as low energy consumption, efficient waste elimination and a preference for sustainable, plant-based diets, they serve as ambassadors for eco-friendly living practices.
- **PHARMA FRENCHIES:** Bioengineered to produce therapeutic compounds in their saliva, offering natural remedies for common ailments. Their licks provide soothing relief for minor injuries and ailments, making them beloved healers in households worldwide.

GLOSSARY

archaeological—relating to archaeology, the scientific study of examining very old things, like buildings, tools and bones, to better understand how people lived in the past

body language—nonverbal communication that uses movement, facial expressions and gestures. Both animals and humans use it. More than half of what humans say is expressed without words

breed standards—a set of traits considered ideal for a particular breed, including size, color, weight, size and shape of ears and tail, and temperament. Standards vary from country to country and are by no means scientific.

canine—of or relating to the family Canidae, which includes dogs, wolves, coyotes, dingoes and foxes

carbon dating—a scientific process that helps researchers get a rough idea of the age of an ancient object

carnivorous—feeding mostly on meat

cells—the microscopic building blocks that make up every living thing

chromosomes—long, threadlike strands of DNA inside cells. Chromosomes carry information about the organism in genes. A cell has two sets of 23 chromosomes, each set inherited from the biological parents. See *genes* and *DNA*.

coevolution—the process of two or more species that share the same environment and interact a lot evolving together.

conquistadors—a Spanish word referring to the Spanish and Portuguese soldiers who invaded and occupied Central and Southern America

crossbreed—when two different species, like dogs and wolves, can mate and produce offspring

DNA—deoxyribonucleic (dee-OCK-see-ri-bo-new-KLEE-ik) acid, the material found in cells that carries your genetic information, determining how you look, think and feel. See *chromosomes* and *genes*.

enzymes—special chemicals in our bodies that help us to things like digest food and fight off infections

evolution—the process of living things changing over long periods of time as they adapt to changes in their environments

false fox—a genus of canids that look similar to foxes but are genetically different

feral—once domesticated but now wild

fertile/infertile—capable of having offspring (fertile) or incapable of doing so (infertile)

genes—tiny segments of DNA that determine how an individual member of a species looks and acts. We all have 20,000 to 25,000 different genes. See *DNA*.

genetic engineering/gene editing—genetic engineering uses scientific processes to change the chemical information in a gene. For example, some types of corn have been genetically engineered to withstand colder temperatures, which expands their growing season. Gene editing is a special kind of genetic engineering through which scientists make precise changes to a gene.

gene pool—the collective set of genes found within a single reproducing population or species

habitat—the place where a plant or animal naturally lives and grows

herbivores—animals that eat mostly plants

hominoids—the family of animals with humanlike traits. The family includes living animals like humans, great apes and monkeys and extinct species like the Neanderthals.

Homo sapiens—the scientific name for humans, from the Latin words *homo* (human being) and *sapien* (thinking)

hormone—a special chemical in our bodies that acts like a messenger, traveling through the blood stream to send information from one part of the body to another

inbreeding—when closely related animals or plants produce offspring

naturalist—a person who studies plants, animals and other parts of nature

mutation—a change in the DNA of a living thing. Mutations can happen naturally because of body processes, or they can be caused by things like sunlight or chemicals. Most mutations don't have much effect, but some can cause changes in how an organism looks or behaves. For example, a mutation might cause a flower to be a different color or an animal to have a unique trait. Mutation is an important part of evolution.

mutualistic relationships—relationships in which two organisms of different species provide things to each other that allow both of them to live and thrive

nomadic—constantly roaming from place to place, usually to follow food sources or avoid harsh weather

neurological—relating to the nervous system, which includes the brain, spinal cord and all the nerves in your body

Paleolithic—relating to a time in history when humans used tools and weapons made of stone and lived by hunting animals and gathering wild plants for food. The period started around 2.5 to 3 million years ago and lasted until about 12,000 BCE.

pedigree—a written record of a specific animal's family tree

purebreds—animals whose parents are members of the same recognized breed

species—a group of animals that are closely related and share a high number of genetic traits

theory—an idea or set of ideas that explains facts or events or other aspects of life

RESOURCES

PRINT

Barr, Catherine, and Steve Williams. *The Story of Life: A First Book about Evolution.* Frances Lincoln Children's Books, 2015.

Church, Dana L. *Animal Minds: What Are They Thinking?* Orca Book Publishers, 2024.

Flaherty, William. *Arctic Wolves*. Inhabit Media, 2018.

Groc, Isabelle. *Conservation Canines: How Dogs Work for the Environment.* Orca Book Publishers, 2021.

Harari, Yuval Noah. *Unstoppable Us, Volume 1: How Humans Took Over the World.* Puffin Canada, 2022.

Hirsch, Andy. *Science Comics: Dogs: From Predator to Protector.* First Second, 2017.

Koonoo, Brian. *Arctic Fox.* Inhabit Media, 2023.

ONLINE

Brains On: brainson.org
A podcast that explores scientific topics in an engaging manner. Search for episodes like "Evolution: How We Got Here and Where We're Going," which explores the basics of evolution and natural selection.

Crash Course Kids: complexly.com/shows/crash-course-kids
A YouTube video series that makes complex scientific concepts accessible and interesting for kids. Search for episodes like "Why Human Evolution Matters," which delves into the importance of human evolution and how understanding our evolutionary past can provide insights into our future.

Earth Rangers: earthrangers.com
A cool podcast about animals and their environment.

National Geographic Kids: kids.nationalgeographic.com
Check out their YouTube channel to find videos like "The Evolution of Dogs," a video about how wolves became dogs.

SciShow Kids: patreon.com/scishow
A YouTube channel that presents scientific concepts in a fun and educational way. It has a variety of videos on evolution, such as "How Did Dogs Become Our Best Friends?" "What Is Evolution?" and "How Do We Know Evolution Is Real?"

Tumble: A Science Podcast for Kids: sciencepodcastforkids.com
This podcast makes complex scientific topics accessible and fun. Search for episodes like "The Surprising Story of the First Dogs," "The Story of Us: How Humans Evolved" and "The Mystery of the Exploding Ants."

KEVIN KOZICKI/GETTY IMAGES

ACKNOWLEDGMENTS

Thanks to all my friends at Orca Books: Kirstie Hudson, Georgia Bradburne, Troy Cunningham, Vivian Sinclair, Ruth Linka and Andrew Wooldridge.

INDEX

Page numbers in **bold** *indicate an image caption.*

CHRISTOPHER GUDGEON writes books, TV shows and movies. He loves animals and ghost stories and has written a lot on both subjects. His favorite animals are dogs and wolves.

ALBERTO MENENDEZ CERVERO/
GETTY IMAGES